"Science knows no country,
because knowledge belongs to humanity,
and is the torch which illuminates the world."
— Louis Pasteur

The world is my country, all mankind are my brethren,
and to do good is my religion."
— Thomas Paine

"You're capable of such beautiful dreams, and such horrible nightmares.
You feel so lost. So cut off. So alone. Only you're not.

See, in all our searching, the only thing we've found
that makes the emptiness bearable is each other." - Carl Sagan

AnnabelleAndAiden.com
Facebook.com/AnnabelleAndAiden

Annabelle & Aiden
stared at the ground,
at black ants—and red—
and some chocolate-brown!

At ravens and doves,
and crows in the sky,
while tunas and guppies,
and swordfish swam by.

A species is a group of organisms in which any two individuals can produce fertile offspring. That is the guideline, and it's important to understand when discussing evolution.

"There's so **many species** of ants, fish, and birds! They don't live **together**, or roam the same herds.

"But if *people* are related to other life under the sun, why do they have *many* species, while us **humans** just have...one?"

3

"One?!

"Over twenty human species were around, *longer than you!* It may *seem* like you're alone, but that's actually quite new."

In 1974 Ethiopia, researchers discovered 40% of a skeleton of a new species, changing what we know about human evolution forever.

"What?!" Aiden said, "*Other* human-like species?!"

They named her Lucy, since they heard the Beatles' song *Lucy In The Sky With Diamonds* around the time of their discovery.

"Oh, I saw the *whole* thing," said a voice, "My name's Lucy.

4

"The human story starts
like the world's, you should know:
with a loud, *big bang*,
(followed by a big toe.)

Here we go...

5

Once **India** was floating
and it *BANGED* into Asia
and made the tallest mountains
called the Himalayas,

which blocked the rain from reaching
the trees in Africa,
and turned its forests
into an empty savannah.

Climate change and heat
waves also caused the
expansion of the savannah.

AFRICA

6

ARAB

50 million yrs ago, India began colliding into Asia. This continues today, at 10-12 inches a year.

So primates that lived there
ran out of trees to climb!
They did not know how to walk.
They were running out of time.

Early primates had long, curved fingers and toes (with short legs) built for climbing and swinging — certainly not for walking. Bipedalism began 4-7 million yrs ago.

INDIA

BAY OF BENGAL

7

Standing up → narrowed hips → narrowed birth canals
favored early births → longer childhoods →
why humans are born "premature." We are more shaped
by our (early) environment (and less by our genes)
than any other species.

Until one day a baby
was born with something new:
a *flat big toe* on each foot.
She knew what she had to do...

Our big toes support 30% of our weight as we
walk. They make running, jumping,
and much of what we do possible.

She took a step, learned to walk,
stood up straight, (which helped her see),
and had babies that could *walk* as well,
and one of those was me.

Advantages of walking upright: more efficient,
better visual command, less sun on back.

We spread out through Africa,
as *Austra-lo-pith-e-cus*,
and soon we changed again.
We evolved right into this...

East Africa, 3.9 million yrs ago.

AFRICA

9

Many **types** of human species!
Each one learning something new.
Some made **tools** and some made **fire**,
that made food easy to chew.

fire → cooking → smaller jaws
→ less chewing → bigger brains

10

Jaws got smaller, brains got bigger,
as we gazed up at the stars.
We started to make drawings,
as we pondered who we are.

To run and hunt long distance
we lost our fur, to stay cool.
Some humans left Africa.
Others stayed and became...you.

70,000 yrs ago

Many think that in Africa, the Australopithecus
(eventually) became Homo Habilis, who became Erectus,
who became Heidelbergensis. Some Heidelbergensis went
to Europe and became Neanderthals. Some went to Asia
and became Denisovans. The ones that stayed in Africa became
us, Sapiens, who later left Africa and met the other species.

II

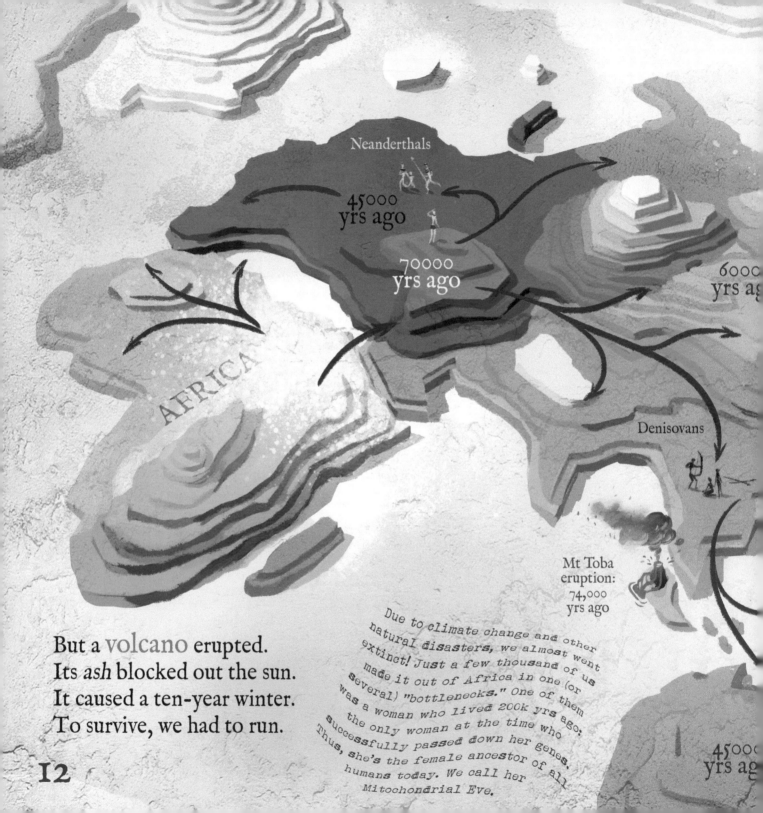

Neanderthals

45000 yrs ago

70000 yrs ago

6000 yrs ag

AFRICA

Denisovans

Mt Toba eruption: 74,000 yrs ago

45000 yrs ag

But a volcano erupted.
Its *ash* blocked out the sun.
It caused a ten-year winter.
To survive, we had to run.

12

Due to climate change and other natural disasters, we almost went extinct! Just a few thousand of us made it out of Africa in one (or several) "bottlenecks." One of them was a woman who lived 200k yrs ago: the only woman at the time who successfully passed down her genes. Thus, she's the female ancestor of all humans today. We call her Mitochondrial Eve.

Just a **few** humans escaped:
just the children of an Eve,
made it to the **northern** lands,
and across the **seven** seas.

As we learned to make clothes to keep us warm...

16000 yrs ago

14000 yrs ago

We found **sloths** twenty feet tall!
Sabre-toothed tigers and huge bears.
Kangaroos over six feet!
Whose teeth gave us quite a scare.

And humans that left Africa
before us: how they had changed!
Into other human species
that were very, very **strange**...

Humans quickly eradicated most all
mammals we came into contact with.

Sthenurine

Megatherium

12000 yrs ago

13

Some were big and some were small.
Some were less than four feet tall!
Hobbits that had lived in caves,
had strange tools and tiny brains.

Homo Floresnsiesis' name reflects the
location of their 2003 discovery: the
island of Flores in Indonesia. These
mysterious "hobbits" stood around 3.5
feet tall, and existed far longer than
our species has, and most amazingly,
overlapped with us. We co-existed! It
seems they went extinct around 50,000 yrs
ago, though a few scientists speculate
they still might exist in remote forests!

Some made axes, some ate meat.
Some built huts to block the heat.
Some could speak, bury their dead,
and hunt large beasts to stay well-fed.

Homo Habilis lived in Africa from 2.3 to 1.4 million yrs ago.

Homo Erectus lived 1.8 million yrs ago, and were the first to make fire and stone hand axes.

We hunted them and ate their food.
They disappeared because
the rest joined our families,
and became a part of us.

15

Today, all humans (except those of African descent) have around 4%
Neanderthal DNA. And humans in East Asia contain DNA of Denisovans (since their
ancestors mated with them).

Traits we could have
picked up from (mating with)
Neanderthals include red hair, broad
noses, rosy cheeks, elongated
skulls, small chins, fair skin,
freckles, large eyes, wide fingers,
nicotine addiction, risk of
long-term depression, blood clots,
and immunity against Eurasian
pathogens.

Do you have red hair or freckles?
Have you gotten rosy cheeks?
That is them still deep inside you.
You still have some of their genes.

16

Our new lands had changed us too:
those that headed farthest east,
where the snow glared bright with sun,
grew narrowed eyes to help them see.

And up north, we needed more
Vitamin D from lack of sun.
So skin got whiter, and we learned how
to drink cow's milk. Oh, what fun.

Our skin color is purely a result
of ultra-violet rays present in
the lands we settled into. Early
humans that headed away from the
equator turned white to get more
Vitamin D from the sun, and were
able to do that since UV rays there
weren't as strong.

MAP OF INDIGENOUS
HUMAN SKIN COLOR

We shared stories, tales, and myths
to explain the unexplained,
and to get along in groups,
and help us cooperate.

We grew feelings of free will,
and of group identity,
and how everyone should act,
which we called morality.

All animals — from ants in a colony, to wolves
in a pack — develop a "feeling" or "sense" of
how all their members should act. Humans, of
course, are no exception. The gods and moral
codes we write throughout our history are a
reflection of our moral compass at the time.

We **wrote** these down sometimes,
or we made them into **art**.
We banged on drums and **danced**,
and we sang them from our heart.

One day a special woman
saw dropped seeds grow into wheat.
So she then invented farming,
and we had much more to eat.

Agriculture began around 11,500 yrs ago in several independent
points of origin including China, Mesopotamia, and the Levant.

20

The woman's task was to gather fruits, seeds and things like honey and eggs (and still is, in today's isolated societies). When preparing her seeds, some would inevitably spill and germinate. She realized that kitchen water thrown in the vicinity would result in those barley or oats looking better than others. Thus agriculture was born.

We tamed peas, lentils, and goats.
Horses, wheat, and olive trees.
We could **settle** in one place,
and build **large** communities.

This was arguably the single most important development for our species: no longer did we have to wander, but we could settle down and establish villages and kingdoms. Now we had extra time to create, invent, and evolve in other ways we never had before.

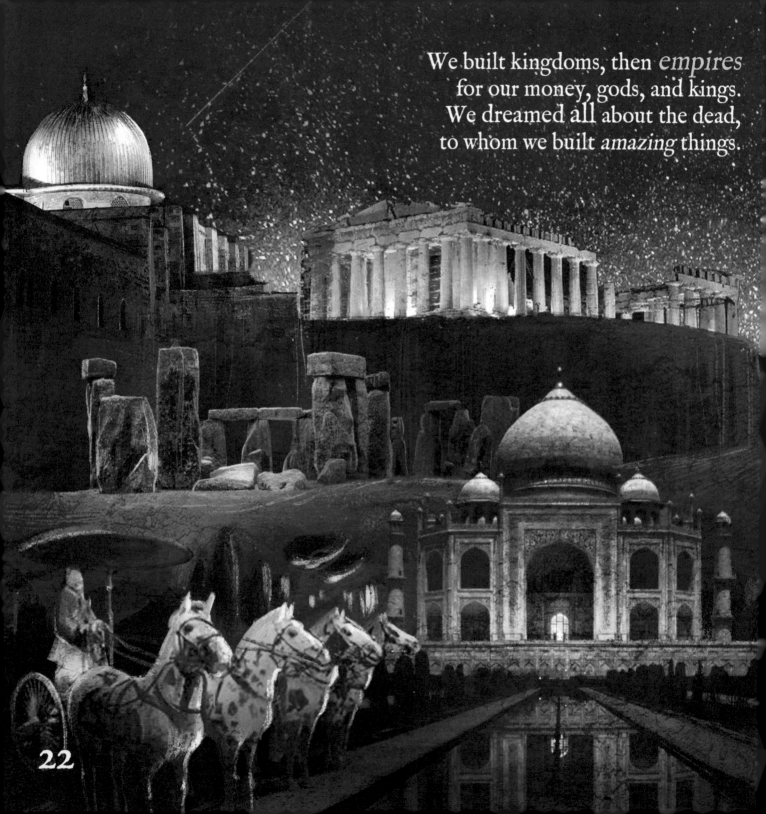

We built kingdoms, then *empires*
for our money, gods, and kings.
We dreamed all about the dead,
to whom we built *amazing* things.

22

But some began to question
if our shared stories were true.
If the world's as small as us,
and the things we thought we knew.

23

One man showed us different:
that we're simply only one
of many different planets that
revolve around the sun.

COPERNICUS

24

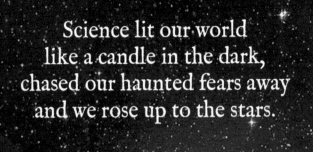

Science lit our world
like a candle in the dark,
chased our haunted fears away
and we rose up to the stars.

We landed on the moon,
split the atom, fought disease.
We tripled our own lifespans,
and found electricity.

We learned we came from stardust,
and all share a family tree.
How our story's deep inside us...
yes, it's written in our genes!

By tradition, the "Scientific Revolution" refers to historical changes that unfolded in Europe between roughly 1550–1700, beginning with Nicholas Copernicus who asserted a heliocentric (sun-centered) cosmos, and ending with Isaac Newton, who proposed universal laws and a Mechanical Universe.

We were hunters and foragers. The frontier was everywhere. We were bounded only by the earth, and the ocean, and the sky. That's home. That's us. On it everyone you love, everyone you know, everyone you ever heard of, every human being who ever was, their lived out lives.

The aggregate of our joy and suffering, thousands of confident religions, ideologies, and economic doctrines, every hunter and forager, every hero and coward, every creator and destroyer of civilization, every king and peasant, every young couple in love, every mother and father, hopeful child, inventor and explorer, every teacher of morals, every corrupt politician, every "superstar," every "supreme leader," every saint and sinner in the history of our species lived there--on a mote of dust suspended in a sunbeam.

they could become the momentary masters of a fraction of a dot. Think of the endless cruelties visited by the inhabitants of one corner of this pixel on the scarcely distinguishable inhabitants of some other corner, how frequent their misunderstandings, how eager they are to kill one another, how fervent their hatreds.

Our posturings, *our imagined self-importance*, the delusion that we have some privileged position in the Universe, are challenged by this

Sapiens! Our story is etched into our DNA along with those of others we picked up along the way.

We're all the same, but different. We're different but the same. We come in different colors, but we share the same name:

26

The Earth is a very small stage in a vast cosmic arena. Think of the rivers of blood spilled by all those generals and emperors so that, in glory and triumph,

point of pale light. Our planet is a lonely speck in the great enveloping cosmic dark. In our obscurity, in all this vastness, there is no hint that help will come from elsewhere to save us from ourselves.

The Earth is the only world known so far to harbor life. There is nowhere else, at least in the near future, to which our species could migrate. Visit, yes. Settle, not yet. Like it or not, for the moment the Earth where we make our stand.

has been said that astronomy is humbling and character-building experience. There is perhaps no better demonstration of the folly of human conceits than this distant image of our tiny world. To me, it underscores our responsibility to deal more kindly with one another,

The open road still softly calls. We, who cannot even put our own planetary home in order, riven with rivalries and hatreds; *are we to venture out* settle even *into space?* By the time we are ready to the nearest other planetary systems, we will have changed.

solar beyond, unified, common their

Our remote descendants, safely arrayed on many worlds through the system, and will be by their heritage, by their regard for their home planet, and by the knowledge that, whatever other life may be, the only humans in all the universe, come from Earth. They will gaze up and strain to find the blue dot in their skies. They will marvel at how vulnerable the repository of all our potential once was, how perilous our infancy, how humble our beginnings, how many rivers we had to cross, before we found our way.

— Carl Sagan

and to preserve and cherish the pale blue dot, the only home we've ever known.

Despite the borders and divisions
we all like to construct,
We are **all** children of Lucy.
We all came from Africa.

27

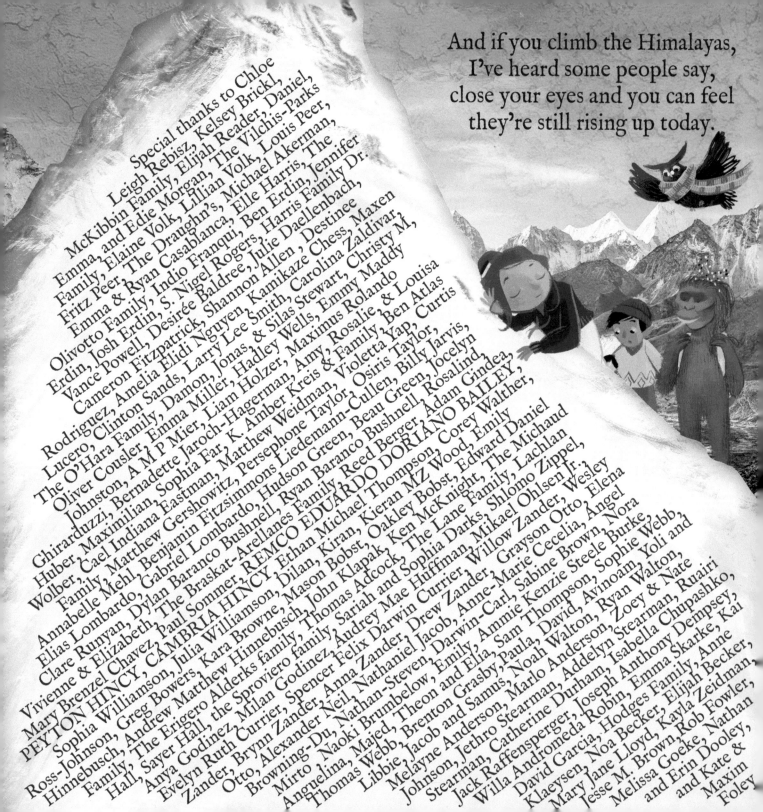

And if you climb the Himalayas,
I've heard some people say,
close your eyes and you can feel
they're still rising up today.

Special thanks to Chloe Leigh Rebisz, Kelsey Brickl, McKibbin Family, Elijah Reader, Daniel, Emma, and Edie Morgan, The Vilchis-Parks Family, Elaine Volk, Lillian Volk, Louis Peer, Fritz Peer, The Draughn's, Michael Akerman, Emma & Ryan Casablanca, Elle Harris, The Olivotto Family, Indio Franqui, Ben Erdin, Jennifer Erdin, Josh Erdin, S. Nigel Rogers, Harris Family, Vance Powell, Desirée Baldree, Julie Daellenbach, Cameron Fitzpatrick, Shannon Allen, Destinee Rodriguez, Amelia Elidi Nguyen, Kamikaze Chess, Maxen Lucero, Clinton Sands, Larry Lee Smith, Carolina Zaldivar, The O'Hara Family, Damon, Jonas, & Silas Stewart, Christy M, Oliver Cousler, Emma Miller, Hadley Wells, Emmy Maddy Johnston, A M P Mier, Liam Holzer, Maximus Rolando Ghirarduzzi, Bernadette Jaroch-Hagerman, Amy, Rosalie, & Louisa Huber, Maximilian, Sophia Far, K. Amber Kreis & Family, Ben Atlas Wolber, Cael Indiana Eastman, Matthew Weidman, Violetta Yap, Curtis Annabelle Mehl, Benjamin Fitzsimmons Liedemann-Cullen, Billy Jarvis, Elias Lombardo, Dylan Baranco Bushnell, Ryan Baranco Bushnell, Rosalind, Clare Runyan, Greg Bowers, Hudson Green, Beau Green, Jocelyn Johnson, Andrew Matthew Hinnebusch, Persephone Taylor, Osiris Taylor, Family, The Erigero Alderks family, Paul Sommer, REMCO EDUARDO DORIANO BAILEY, Hall, Sayer Hall, the Sproviero family, The Braskat-Arellanes Family, Reed Berger, Adam Gindea, Anya Godinez, Milan Godinez, Ethan Michael Thompson, Corey Walther, Evelyn Ruth Currier, Spencer Felix Darwin Currier, Dilan, Kiran, Kieran MZ Wood, Emily Zander, Brynn Zander, Anna Zander, Mason Bobst, Oakley Bobst, Edward Daniel Otto, Alexander Neil, Nathaniel Jacob, John Klapak, Ken McKnight, The Michaud Browning-Du, Naoki Brumbelow, Thomas Adcock, The Lane Family, Lachlan Mirto, Majed, Theon and Elia, Sariah and Sophia Darks, Shlomo Zippel, Anguelina, Jacob and Samus, Audrey Mae Huffman, Mikael Ohlsen Jr., Thomas Webb, Brenton Steven, Drew Zander, Willow Zander, Wesley Libbie, Jacob Darwin-Carl, Anne-Marie Cecelia, Grayson Otto, Elena Melayne Anderson, Marlo Anderson, Sam Thompson, Sophie Webb, Johnson, Jethro Stearman, Emily, Ammie Kenzie Steele Burke, Stearman, Catherine Durham, Addelyn Stearman, Ryan Walton, Grasby, Paula, David, Avinoam, Zoey & Nate Jack Raffensperger, Joseph Anthony Dempsey, Willa Andromeda Robin, Emma Skarke, Kai Noah Walton, Yoli and David Garcia, Hodges Family, Isabella Chupashko, Klaeysen, Noa Becker, Elijah Becker, Mary Jane Lloyd, Kayla Zeidman, Jesse M. Brown, Rob Fowler, Melissa Goeke, Nathan and Erin Dooley, Maxim and Kate & Foley

Vivienne & Elizabeth, Mary Brenzel Chavez, PEYTON HINCY, CAMBRIA HINCY, Ross-Johnson, Hinnebusch, Sophia Williamson, Julia Williamson, Kara Browne,

CPSIA information can be obtained
at www.ICGtesting.com
Printed in the USA
BVHW021201100319
541605BV00003B/1/P